EAST RENFREWSHIRE COUNCIL

0558146X

D0854332

The United Kingdom *Today*

The United Kingdom *Today*

Michael Gallagher

FRANKLIN WATTS
LONDON•SYDNEY

Designer Peter Bailey/Proof Books
Editor Constance Novis
Art Director Jonathan Hair
Editor-in-Chief John C. Miles
Picture research Sarah Smithies

Copyright © Franklin Watts 2006

Franklin Watts
338 Euston Road
London NW1 3BH

Franklin Watts Australia
Hachette Children's Books
Level 17/207 Kent Street
Sydney NSW 2000

All rights reserved

A CIP catalogue record for this book
is available from the British Library

Dewey classification number: 914.1

ISBN-10: 0 7496 6488 6
ISBN-13: 978 0 7496 6488 6

Printed in China

EAST RENFREWSHIRE COUNCIL	
0558146	
Bertrams	22.12.06
J941	£12.99

Franklin Watts is a division of Hachette Children's Books.

Picture credits

Inside: Andrew Milligan, Reuters, Corbis: 12. Benedict Luxmoore, Arcaid, Alamy: 31.
British Library, The Art Archive: 6. Chris Barry, Rex Features: 37.
Dagli Orti, A, Fine Art Museum Bilbao, The Art Archive: 16. David Noton Photography, Alamy: 21 (t).
David Poole, Alamy: 18 (b). David Robertson, Alamy: 21(c). Derek Croucher, Corbis: 20.
Gary Merrin , Rex Features: 32. Gianni Muratore , Alamy: 29 (b). GPU, Rex Features: 11.
Greenshoots Communications, Alamy: 40.Hideo Kurihara, Alamy: 22 (l). HL Studios: 46. ICIMAGE, Alamy: 9.
Janine Wiedel Photolibrary, Alamy:19 (b), 36. Jason Smalley, Wildscape, Alamy: 38.
Jayne Fincher, Photo Int, Alamy: 13. JLImages , Alamy: 28-29. John Robertson, Alamy: 26.
Leslie Garland Picture Library, Alamy: 30. Linda Burgess, Alamy: 19 (t). Mary Evans Picture Library, Alamy: 17.
nagelestock.com, Alamy: 24. Peter MacDiarmid, Rex Features: 34. Philippe Hays, Rex Features: 33.
Popperfoto, Alamy: 23 (r). Randy Faris, Corbis: 42. Richard Clune, Corbis: 8. Richard Gardner, Rex Features: 39.
Robin Sanders, Alamy: 27. Sam Morgan Moore, Rex Features: 41. Scott Hortop, Alamy: 18 (c).
Scottish Viewpoint, Alamy: 10. Shout, Rex Features: 43. Sipa Press, Rex Features : 25, 35. Superbild, A1pix: 3, 7.
The Hoberman Collection, Alamy: 15. The Photolibrary Wales, Alamy: 22-23 (c). Visual Arts Library (London), Alamy: 14.

Cover: Front: David Aubrey, Corbis (bc). Jose Fuste Raga, Corbis (br). Richard Clune, Corbis (bl). Superbild, A1pix (t),
Back: Corbis. Superbild, A1pix (b).

*Every attempt has been made to clear copyright. Should there be any
inadvertent omission please apply to the publisher for rectification.*

Contents

Introduction

Few countries can boast the United Kingdom's wealth of history and tradition. But today, the British are also modernising fast.

Islands united

Due to the complications of geography, politics and culture, many people confuse the terms Britain, United Kingdom and British Isles and, in particular, there is often confusion over exactly what the United Kingdom (or UK) is. To be precise, Great Britain refers only to the island containing three separate countries: England, Scotland and Wales. It does not include the province of Northern Ireland, across the Irish Sea. Together though, Great Britain and Northern Ireland make up the state known as the United Kingdom, whose citizens call themselves British. Hundreds of smaller islands such as Anglesey and the Scottish Hebrides also belong to the United Kingdom. The entire group of islands, including Ireland, is known as the British Isles, but this is a geographical term only and does not mean that they are all British possessions.

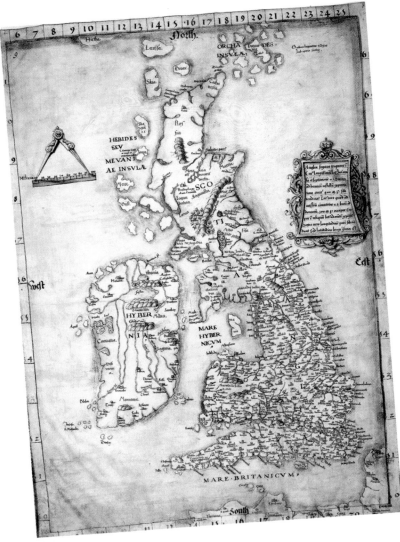

The island of Great Britain – shown in this 16th-century map – contains only England, Scotland and Wales.

'This precious stone set in the silver sea, Which serves it in the office of a wall... Against the envy of less happier lands.'

WILLIAM SHAKESPEARE (1564-1616), PLAYWRIGHT, DESCRIBES ENGLAND

Imperial might

For centuries, the British considered themselves lucky to be islanders, since this helped keep foreign enemies out and enabled seaborne trade to flourish. Indeed, by 1850 the UK had become the most powerful state in the world. It had an empire so big that the sun never set on all of it, and by the nineteenth century it was the number one industrial and military power. Today, the UK is no longer so influential, although it has developed a more tolerant and diverse society.

Strength in diversity

The British may have lost their empire, but they have allowed some former colonial subjects to immigrate, and embraced their cultures in the process. Among the native British themselves, a minority of people speak traditional languages like Scots, Gaelic and Welsh. And some people even find it difficult to understand the English spoken in numerous regional dialects. However, this variety is reflected in the UK's success in the arts, fashion and design.

Many traditional industrial areas have fallen on hard times, yet the economy remains one of the world's biggest. Today the southeast of England is one of the richest regions in Europe – with a very high cost of living to match.

The United Kingdom's Union Flag. Technically it can only be called a 'Jack' when flown from the jack-staff of a ship.

Symbol of unity: the Union Flag

The United Kingdom's national flag is called the Union Flag but is also known as the Union Jack. It is actually three flags in one, representing the union of England and Wales with Scotland and Northern Ireland. The flag of England (a red cross on a white background) is superimposed on the Scottish saltire (a white diagonal cross on a blue background) and the Irish cross of Saint Patrick (a red diagonal cross on a white background). The Welsh dragon does not appear on the flag, because at the time that the Union Jack was designed, Wales was considered to be part of England.

GEOGRAPHY			POLITICS	
	Location	Island	Status	Nationality of citizens
ENGLAND	British Isles	Great Britain	Part of UK	British
SCOTLAND	British Isles	Great Britain	Part of UK	British
WALES	British Isles	Great Britain	Part of UK	British
N. IRELAND	British Isles	Ireland	Part of UK	British and/or Irish
REPUBLIC OF IRELAND	British Isles	Ireland	Independent republic	Irish
CHANNEL ISLANDS	British Isles	Channel Islands	UK crown dependency	British
ISLE OF MAN	British Isles	Isle of Man	UK crown dependency	British

Geography: Shaped by the seas

Thanks to its location, the UK enjoys a gentle climate and fine scenery, all close to mainland Europe.

Warming effect

The British Isles sit just off the north-west coast of Europe, between Scandinavia and the Atlantic Ocean. Their northerly location would make for a very cold climate were it not for the curious ocean current known as the gulf stream, which brings warmer waters from the Caribbean, helping to raise temperatures and making extreme weather a rarity. Even so, UK weather is notoriously unpredictable. Mild winds from the south can give way to icy blasts from the east, then wet fronts from the Atlantic – sometimes, it seems, all in one day!

The cool, damp climate of the UK produces lush green landscapes such as this one, in Yorkshire.

Subtle beauty

Like the weather, the UK's landscape is not highly dramatic, but it is diverse. There are no mighty rivers or spectacular mountain ranges. Yet it is still a place of great beauty. From the chalky soils of southern England, which rise up in the famous white cliffs at Dover, to the craggy highlands of Scotland, there is huge variety. And because of the climate, much of the land is very fertile. Tiny, picturesque farming villages still exist alongside major cities and smaller market towns. Many British people dream of living in the countryside, although today, the population is overwhelmingly urban.

The Channel Tunnel

In 1994, the British ceased to be an island race, with the opening of their first-ever land link to Europe. Costing £10 billion to build, the Channel Tunnel is 50 kilometres long and carries trains 40 metres below the seabed of the English Channel – one of the world's busiest shipping routes. Passengers can now speed from London to Paris and Brussels in less than three hours, or transport their cars (above) from Great Britain to the French coast in around half an hour.

Uncertain position

Nowhere in the United Kingdom is more than 120 kilometres from the sea, and for centuries, the UK was a great naval power. Nowadays though, most people's experience of maritime life is limited to a trip on one of the many ferries that connect Great Britain to neighbouring islands and the rest of Europe.

At its narrowest point, the European mainland is only around 35 kilometres away from the English coast. But this proximity, combined with the UK's cultural and physical separation, has contributed to an identity crisis among some Britons. Should they forge closer links with their European neighbours, or with English-speaking North America? Or should the UK return to being a completely separate power? It is a question which, so far, the nation has yet to answer.

FACTFILE : THE UK

Full name: The United Kingdom of Great Britain and Northern Ireland

Location (London): 51°N, 0°W

Total area: 244,755 square km

International land borders: 360 km (with Republic of Ireland)

Coastline: 12,429 km

Longest river: River Severn (354 km)

Highest elevation: 1343 m above sea level (Ben Nevis, Scotland)

Lowest elevation: -4 m below sea level (the Fens, eastern England)

Highest village: 465 m above sea level (Flash, Staffordshire)

Average rainfall: 610 mm

Average Summer temperature, 2003:
Northern Scotland: 11.6° Celsius
SE England: 15.3° Celsius

Average Winter temperature, 2003:
Northern Scotland: 4.5° Celsius
SE England: 6.5° Celsius

MAJOR CITIES & POPULATION:

London, England (capital)	7,172,000
Birmingham, England	971,000
Glasgow, Scotland	630,000
Liverpool, England	469,000
Leeds, England	443,000
Edinburgh, Scotland (capital)	430,000
Manchester, England	394,000
Cardiff, Wales (capital)	292,000
Belfast, Northern Ireland (capital)	277,000

People: Celebrating difference

The British are descended from the many peoples who have settled, invaded and migrated to their land over the centuries; a process that continues today.

Mixed race

Little is known about the earliest inhabitants of Great Britain. They are thought to have been hunter-gatherers who probably arrived following the northward retreat of ice after the last Ice Age, around 10,000 years ago. Much later though, the Celts, the Romans, the Germanic Angles and Saxons, the Vikings and, lastly, in 1066, the Normans of what is now northern France, invaded Great Britain. Today's native population therefore contains a rich genetic mixture, with ancestral links to some of the native populations of continental Europe.

Celtic fringe

According to popular history, the ancient Britons of the Iron Age were Celts, many of whom were driven westwards by Germanic invaders after the Romans left Great Britain around 1600 years ago. To this day, some British people talk of a western 'Celtic fringe' made up of Wales, Scotland, Ireland and the extreme tip of southwestern England, whose inhabitants believe they differ from the English.

The cultural distinctiveness of the Celtic fringe is most evident in the survival of Gaelic-based languages in Northern Ireland, Wales, Scotland and the Isle of Man. And, there is still much good-humoured rivalry between the 'Celts' – especially the fiercely free-spirited Scots – and the English.

Meanwhile, UK society in general is becoming more mixed amidst another influx of newcomers.

In parts of Scotland, the Gaelic language is in everyday use. This picture shows a postman in front of a post office in the Outer Hebrides.

A modern UK city street scene includes people of all races and colours; recent immigrants as well as those whose families have been in the country for generations.

Melting pot

Immigration from the Commonwealth during the twentieth century has brought people of many racial backgrounds to all regions of the UK. The big cities, in particular, have become a magnet for new arrivals, keen to be part of the country's relatively tolerant society. Larger ethnic minorities now include people of Irish, West Indian, south Asian and African backgrounds.

In addition, the UK plays its part in offering refuge to those fleeing persecution all over the world. In the last ten years, immigration of all kinds has contributed to one-half of the UK's population growth and today, up to 2.6 million inhabitants describe themselves as Muslim, while substantial Jewish, Hindu and other religious minorities are also thriving. As a whole though, the population is ageing, with more than one in six people now over the age of 65. There is a debate over how many immigrants might be needed in future, to top up the workforce.

> 'A mongrel half-bred race.'
>
> – DANIEL DEFOE (1660-1731),
> NOVELIST, ON THE ENGLISH

THE UK PEOPLE IN FIGURES
(2004 ESTIMATES)

Population		
England: 50,093,100	(83.7%)
Scotland: 5,078,400	(8.5%)
Wales: 2,952,500	(4.9%)
Northern Ireland: 1,710,300	(2.9%)
Total UK: 59,834,300	

Average population growth: 0.4% per year
Average age: 38.6 years
Life expectancy: 75.7 years (male),
80.7 years (female)

Europe's eastern promise

When the European Union admitted 10 new member states in 2004 some people feared a very large influx of immigrants into the UK, legally entitled to settle and search for work. In fact, arrivals from former communist states like Poland and the Czech Republic have been less than expected, with around 123,000 people granted work permits in the first year of EU expansion. Many have brought much-needed skills in areas like medicine and construction.

Politics: A people empowered

The Queen is the head of state of the United Kingdom. Real authority, however, lies in the hands of politicians – and not all of them are based in London.

Royalty restrained

The United Kingdom is a constitutional monarchy, which means that power is shared between a hereditary monarch and an elected government. Both must observe a supreme body of law called a constitution.

The government is led by a prime minister and a so-called cabinet of ministers who between them are responsible for major issues like health, defence and foreign policy. It rules in the name of the monarch, currently Queen Elizabeth II, and her influence is restricted to offering consultations, warnings and advice. However, ministers may be foolish to ignore these, because the Queen has now reigned for over half a century. This makes her much more experienced than any elected politician.

A view of the Scottish parliament. In recent years government has moved away - 'devolved' – from Westminster.

Parliament supreme

The government must also answer to parliament, which sits in two chambers. Members of the lower chamber, the House of Commons, are elected. The upper chamber, the House of Lords, was traditionally made up of hereditary peers. Today, most of its members are appointed in the name of the Queen. Both chambers are located at the Palace of Westminster (also simply called Westminster).

The House of Commons contained 646 elected Members of Parliament (or, MPs for short) after the 2005 general election. The government must convince a majority of these MPs to give their support in order to pass a new law. The new law is then considered by the House of Lords, which may ask for alterations or even withhold approval.

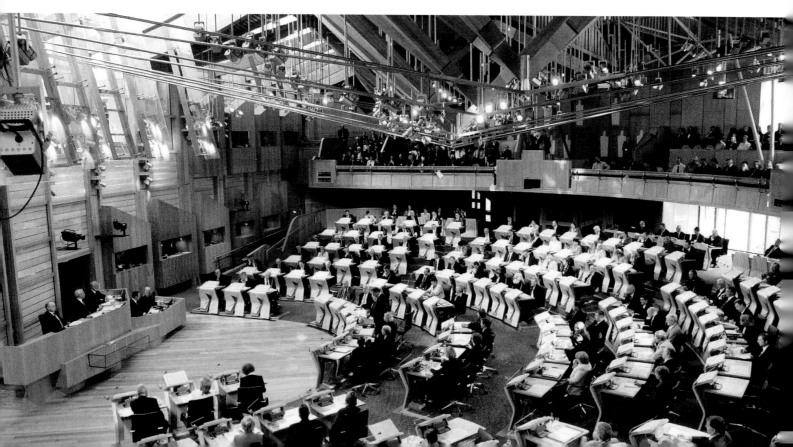

Spreading the power

Parliament has governed for centuries from the Palace of Westminster. However, several years ago, major changes were made to parliament, in a process known as devolution. Certain powers were devolved (passed on) to two new chambers – a Scottish parliament in Edinburgh and a Welsh assembly in Cardiff – in order to give Scotland and Wales more influence over the running of their own affairs. (Amidst some difficulty, devolution has also been attempted in Northern Ireland.)

In practice, devolution means that many issues exclusive to these countries can be dealt with locally, rather than in London. Some people see devolution as a stepping-stone to full Scottish and Welsh independence from the UK.

'England is the mother of parliaments.'

JOHN BRIGHT (1811-89), BRITISH STATESMAN

The European question

The UK is a member state of the European Union (EU), and this, too, involves the British government giving up some of its power. Certain laws, especially relating to trade, are passed by the European parliament in Strasbourg and Brussels, and applied across the EU. In return, all 25 EU members can easily export their goods to one another.

Some British people believe Europe has too much influence. The UK chose not to adopt the European single currency, known as the euro. And the extent to which the country should allow the EU to control its affairs has become a highly-charged political question.

The Queen, as Head of State, opens parliament in an elaborate ceremony every November.

Pomp and power: the state opening of parliament

Each session of the British parliament is opened in a ceremony led by the Queen. Dressed in majestic robes, she arrives at Westminster in a horse-drawn carriage. Politicians and invited guests assemble in the House of Lords to hear her deliver a speech. The speech has been prepared by ministers, and outlines the government's agenda. The event is full of historic rituals. For example, a government official is held at Buckingham Palace as a symbolic hostage for the monarch's safe return, echoing the days when monarchs and elected politicians vied with each other for power.

History: Forging the nation

The British nation grew out of the union of England Scotland and Wales, and the story of its development is one of war, trade and religious solidarity.

Wales incorporated

Britain's formal unification is relatively recent, stretching back only a few centuries. The first so-called Act of Union was passed in 1536, during the reign of King Henry VIII, and began the integration of Wales into England. At that time most of Wales was already under the control of the English king. But Henry had just declared himself leader of the Church of England, thwarting the power of the Roman Catholic Pope, based in Rome. Worried that forces loyal to the Pope might use Wales as a springboard to invade England, he decided to increase his control over it. The semi-independent border estates, known as the Welsh Marches, were converted into counties, and were represented in the English parliament. Then, all of Wales was made subject to English law, and English was made the main language, with the native Welsh tongue relegated to second-class status.

Troubled union

In 1707, another Act of Union was passed by the parliaments of England and Scotland. This replaced both bodies with a single British parliament, based in London, and created the United Kingdom of Great Britain. England and Scotland had different reasons for uniting. The English wanted to prevent a Scottish Roman Catholic becoming King, while the Scottish wanted to gain access to English colonies and the more powerful English economy. The Scots were also granted considerable financial incentives to unite. And, to accommodate them further, the Scottish Church and legal system were left in place. But many ordinary people were still opposed to the union.

A key factor holding the United Kingdom together throughout the 18th century was the need to oppose the armies of Roman Catholic France. This painting shows the French victory at the battle of Denain in 1712.

Britannia: Beauty and power personified

Britannia was the Romans' name for their colony in Britain. It was represented on coins by the figure of a goddess-like woman. This human image of Britain was revived in the eighteenth century (right) to celebrate the new nation, and has survived to this day. Britannia holds a trident and a shield, and is usually depicted in robes and a helmet. The British lion often sits at her feet, which are lapped by waves, symbolising Britain's naval power.

Common interest

After 1707, the idea of a common British identity gained strength only because each country could see the benefits in it. In particular, they were all enriched by advantages of having an empire in the eighteenth and nineteenth centuries. And continuous military threats from Roman Catholic Europe – especially France – knit the Protestant UK ever closer together.

In 1801, yet another Act of Union brought the Irish into the UK, again in response to fears of invasion, though in the twentieth century, most of Ireland became an independent republic. Today, of course, neither the invasion fears nor the empire exist. As a result, a minority of people have begun to question the need to call themselves British, as opposed to English, Scottish, Welsh or Irish.

TIMELINE: THE QUEST FOR UNITY

1534: Act of Supremacy makes King Henry VIII head of the Church of England

1536-43: Acts of Union incorporate Wales into England

1603: James VI of Scotland inherits the English throne. Rules as James I of England

1607: Unsuccessful attempt by James I to formalise a union between Scotland and England

1707: Act of Union between England and Scotland creates a unified British state

1793: Start of wars against revolutionary France

1801: Act of Union with Ireland

1921: Irish Free State established (later the Republic of Ireland). Northern Ireland remains part of the UK

'We are no longer kept together by the need to fight wars, we are no longer all Protestants and we do not have the self-interest of belonging to a massive global empire.'

LINDA COLLEY, BRITISH HISTORIAN, 1992

History: Empire and industry

The British became the most powerful and wealthy nation in the world, thanks to a combination of technical ingenuity and military might.

Industrial revolution

In 1815, the UK's defeat of its greatest enemy, France, at the Battle of Waterloo, enabled British colonial influence to spread around the globe unchallenged. By the late nineteenth century, one-quarter of the world's people lived within the British Empire. Over the same period, the UK economy was transformed. Central to this was the development of an efficient steam engine by Scotsman, James Watt (1736–1819), in the late eighteenth century. Small-scale manufacturing – already expanding – now grew more rapidly than ever. Big steam-powered factories churned out iron goods, textiles and other products that had previously been made by people working from home. Steam also powered railways and ships, allowing goods to be transported more easily. The massive British Empire provided cheap raw materials for UK industry, as well as a place for the UK to sell its manufactured goods.

The Industrial Revolution's advances in industry, such as the iron-making shown here, helped the UK to become a world power.

A nation enslaved

British industrial and imperial riches did not, however, go unnoticed. In the nineteenth century, Germany emerged as a new European rival, seeking to compete with the UK in a hostile rivalry. This eventually led to the horrors of the First World War.

But even during peacetime, the industrial revolution had drawbacks. It could provide higher-paid jobs than those in agriculture, but it often condemned the workers to long hours in the brutal conditions of the factories. And giant, ugly cities, full of chimneys belching smoke and terrible slums, scarred the landscape. For decades until the introduction of limited reforms in the Victorian era, many poorer Britons must have felt more like victims of their country's success, not its beneficiaries.

Sugar Trade.

The import of sugar, produced on overseas plantations worked by slave labour, helped many British ports to become wealthy in the 18th century.

The slave trade

One of the more unsavoury aspects of British economic development was the slave trade. Millions of Africans were shipped from their homes to the Americas and forced to work as domestics in houses or labourers in the fields and on plantations. Often, they were exchanged for products like cotton, which were sold back in Britain or turned into manufactured goods, to buy yet more slaves. Port cities like Liverpool and Bristol grew fabulously wealthy on the proceeds, and some historians believe slavery underpinned the UK's early industrial growth.

'In the best cases a temporarily endurable existence...in the worst cases, bitter want, reaching even homelessness and death by starvation.'

FRIEDRICH ENGELS (1820-1895), GERMAN POLITICAL PHILOSOPHER, COMMENTING ON THE ENGLISH INDUSTRIAL WORKING CLASS IN 1844

Service economy

Since then, the UK economy has undergone a second revolution. Due to foreign competition, heavy industries, such as coal mining and shipbuilding, all but disappeared in the late twentieth century. In addition, manufacturing has diminished considerably and today, more Britons than ever work in so-called service industries like finance, retailing and leisure.

Some people argue that these types of jobs are less secure than the ones they have replaced. But they are generally much cleaner, and safer too. And thanks in part to the lead it established more than 200 years ago, the United Kingdom remains one of the world's biggest exporters of both goods and services.

TIMELINE: THE RISE OF EMPIRE AND INDUSTRY

1712:	First commercially successful steam engine built by Thomas Newcomen. Used to pump water out of coal mines
1763:	Britain and her allies defeat the French in North America
1772:	Extensive canal building begins
1775:	James Watt's improved steam engine
1783:	Loss of Britain's American colonies
1805:	Battle of Trafalgar: Britain gains naval supremacy after defeating the French fleet
1812:	First 'Luddite' riots: impoverished artisans sabotage machinery
1815:	Defeat of Napoleon at Battle of Waterloo
1830:	World's first passenger railway opens between Liverpool and Manchester
1846:	Repeal of Corn Laws introduces free trade
1851:	The Great Exhibition: the UK shows off its world lead in manufacturing

England

England is the UK's dominant country in terms of population and economic might. But few people seem to know what it really means to be English.

English – or British?

One explanation is that the English, as leading players in Britain, have ploughed their self-respect into a wider British nationality instead. Today, that may be changing, as the UK becomes less centralised and each country takes more control of its own affairs. Some English people observe nationalism in Northern Ireland, Scotland and Wales, and want to respond by strengthening their own separate cultural identity. Others complain that they pay more in tax and receive less government spending than the rest of the UK. Now, for the first time in centuries, the flag of Saint George has become popular again. The English may at last be stirring. And some people fear that a more assertive England could spell problems for the smaller countries of the UK.

North-South divide

Well over three-quarters of all UK citizens live in England, but the country is so regionally diverse that some inhabitants can look upon others as virtual foreigners. Accents, attitudes and even lifestyles can differ greatly. One popular stereotype is that those from the south tend to think of themselves as cultured and refined, while northerners are more likely to be working class. There may be little truth in this, but it stems from the undeniable fact that most heavy industry in England was based in the urban midlands and north, while London and the southeast have traditionally formed a wealthier political and administrative region. Today the north-south economic divide remains a matter for some concern. Meanwhile, the east and west of England are overwhelmingly rural.

Two English city stereotypes: the leafy suburban south and the grim industrial north. In reality there is wealth and poverty in both areas and, recently, northern cities have become prosperous after decades of industrial decline.

Defining the English identity

Despite the struggle to find a single identity, there are some cultural traits that the English like to think of as their own. These include a notion of fair play, as enshrined in the typically English game of cricket, an ability to laugh at oneself and a cool, reserved personality.

In 2006 a government-sponsored poll found that the most popular symbols of England included the FA Cup, Punch and Judy, and a cup of tea, though – characteristically – many English people had different ideas about their country. Meanwhile, the rich English language lends itself to poetry and prose, and there is justifiable celebration of literary giants such as Shakespeare. Yet few people seem to display much obvious pride in being English. The commemoration of the national patron saint, Saint George's Day, is not even a public holiday.

Is this how the rest of the world sees England? In a recent survey people listed a cup of tea as being symbolic of English culture.

Morris dance: a curious custom

Few things better display English eccentricity than the traditional Morris dance. Dancers (often men, although there are women's Morris sides) leap and step in formation to folk music. They wear bright costumes with bells on their legs, twirl handkerchiefs and clatter wooden sticks together. Morris dancing possibly originated as a celebration of springtime, or even as ritualised combat.

Scotland

The most northerly country in Great Britain looks warily upon its southern neighbour England, and prides itself on being different.

Rugged beauty

In many ways Scotland feels like a big country, with its breathtaking landscape of mountains, lochs and far-flung islands. Only 8.5 per cent of British people are Scottish but they are a proud and fiercely individual people. Living so far north, the climate they experience is often harsh by UK standards, and the people have developed a reputation for being just as tough as their weather. Even the Romans, who invaded Britain in the 1st Century CE, were unable to subdue the Scots. Indeed, the Roman emperor Hadrian had to build a giant wall to keep the Scots out of his colony to the south.

A view of the skyline of the Scottish capital Edinburgh.

Anything but English

Today, the Scots are once again asserting themselves, albeit peacefully. A nationalist minority believes Scotland's future lies in independence from the rest of the United Kingdom. But even those who support the Union love nothing better than getting the better of their old rivals, the English – especially on the football or rugby field. Such sparring, though, is generally good humoured. In fact, according to tradition, the Scots are committed to social justice to an extent not seen anywhere else in the UK. They have a separate legal and educational system, while the Scottish parliament has tended towards more generous health and welfare policies than those available south of the border.

'The Scottish Parliament, which adjourned on 25 March in the year 1707, is hereby reconvened.'

– WINIFRED EWING, SCOTTISH NATIONALIST, 1999

Scottish Highland scenery includes mountains, lochs (lakes) and heather-covered hills.

Work ethic

The Scots are also known for being particularly hardworking and shrewd, with very noticeable talents for science and engineering. Perhaps it is no surprise then that this is the country which produced the inventors of television and the telephone and, just recently, the scientists who first cloned an animal, Dolly the sheep. Scots also gained a reputation as able colonial administrators in the days of the British Empire.

To many people, though, Scotland means bagpipes, the Highland Games, Hogmanay (New Year) and whisky. With such a strong and distinctive culture, it is easy to think of the country as a single, indivisible unit. However, there are differences within Scottish society, too. In particular, some people in the remote highlands and islands are as wary of Scotland's urban elite as Scots may be of the English!

Burns: Scottish hero

Robert Burns (above), who lived from 1759 to 1796, is the best known of the Scots-language poets, penning such classics as Auld Lang Syne and Tam O'Shanter. A political radical, his works often celebrated the weak and vulnerable in a Scotland that he also depicted as the underdog. Today he remains as a symbol of Scottish culture. His birthday, 25th January, is known as Burns Night. Scots mark it to this day with the ritual 'Burns Supper', comprising readings, toasts and haggis (minced sheep's offal and oatmeal in a casing).

Wales (Cymru)

Wales has been subject to continuous rule from London for over 800 years, but its spirit and customs still flourish.

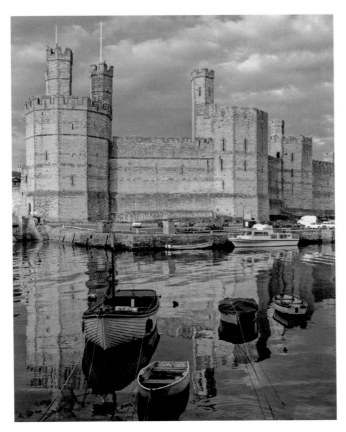

Caernarfon Castle was one of the many fortresses built by English King Edward I when he conquered Wales.

Ancient and modern

Wales is steeped in history. Its mountainous terrain is peppered with mighty castles dating back to the 13th century, when the English King Edward I conquered the country. Yet the Welsh are also a forward-looking people, with renewed self-confidence. Around one-fifth of them now speak Welsh, which is taught alongside English in schools. Most road signs are bilingual, and there is also Welsh-language broadcasting. The Welsh cultural year climaxes in the National Eisteddfod, a Welsh-language literary and arts festival held each August.

Hard times

Life in Wales, though, has sometimes been tough. Most of the population lives in the south, where iron and coal deposits fuelled the growth of heavy industry in the nineteenth century. These areas were then hit hard by economic downturn. Today, almost all the coal mines and heavy industry have gone, and the country has had to diversify into areas like electronics, oil refining and tourism. Meanwhile, much Welsh agricultural land is of relatively poor quality, and suitable only for raising sheep and cattle. The country lies in the path of westerly winds from the Atlantic, making the climate cool and damp.

Quest for justice

Thanks in part to this historic adversity, Welsh people have often been wary of the rich and powerful. They have tended to vote for politicians who support social justice and to follow nonconformist religions like Methodism, which reject pomp and ceremony in favour of more simple worship. One of the most famous Welsh MPs was Aneurin Bevan, who, as the British Health Minister in the 1940s, helped establish the UK's National Health Service.

Since 1999, a devolved assembly has sat in the Welsh capital, Cardiff. However, unlike the Scottish parliament, it does not have tax-raising powers. The Welsh nationalist party, Plaid Cymru, would like to upgrade the assembly, and make Wales an independent country.

Welsh MP Aneurin Bevan, part-founder of the UK's National Health Service in 1948.

> 'Every day when I wake up I thank the Lord I'm Welsh.'
>
> CERYS MATTHEWS,
> WELSH POP SINGER, 1998

Cool Cymru

Wales entered the twenty-first century on an upbeat, thanks to the creation of its devolved assembly but also to an explosion of culture known as Cool Cymru. Led by successful bands such as the Manic Street Preachers and the Stereophonics, it has lit up a country long overshadowed by its English neighbour. And the new Millennium Stadium in Cardiff has given Welsh rugby a spectacular home.

The Manic Street Preachers on stage in Swansea.

Northern Ireland

Northern Ireland – the biggest part of the UK to lie outside Great Britain – offers some spectacular scenery. Its people are trying to overcome the legacies of decades of conflict.

Scenic wonder

Northern Ireland was formed out of six counties of Ireland that did not join the Irish Free State in 1921. Like the rest of Ireland it is largely rural, and known for its landscape. At its centre is a huge lake called Lough Neagh – the largest in the UK. And a spectacular volcanic rock formation called the Giant's Causeway graces the north coast. But despite the beauty of its land, Northern Ireland's recent history has been a difficult one.

Northern Ireland includes some of the UK's most spectacular scenery. The Giant's Causeway, shown here, is a UNESCO World Heritage Site.

Sectarian terror

The problems are often expressed in religious terms, but they really concern Northern Ireland's links with Great Britain. Part of the population is descended from Scottish and English settlers who colonised the region several hundred years ago. These people are overwhelmingly Protestant in faith and see themselves as British. But the remainder of Northern Ireland is Roman Catholic, and wants to belong to the Republic of Ireland.

Paramilitary extremists from the two rival communities unleashed campaigns of violence in the 1970s, which came to be known as the Troubles. Over the next three decades, more than 3,600 people died as a result.

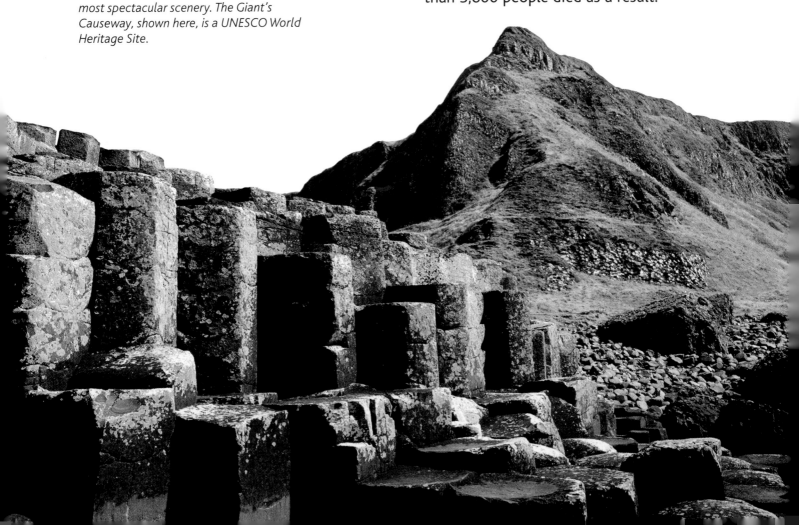

Optimism and obstacles

Today, the Troubles are effectively over, after the main anti-British paramilitary group, the IRA, declared a ceasefire and committed its followers to politics instead. As a result, the province's economy has boomed. Tourism and business, once scared away, have begun to return. Northern Ireland's inhabitants can now choose to be British or Irish citizens, or both. And provision has been made for a devolved assembly to sit at Stormont Castle in Belfast.

But challenges remain. Unemployment is higher than most parts of the UK, and some urban districts remain squalid and uninviting. A number of former paramilitaries have moved into organised crime. And there has been little agreement among politicians on how to move forwards. Northern Ireland may no longer be at war with itself, but the transition to a peaceful, settled society will take time.

Sinn Féin leader Gerry Adams (centre) speaks to the media about the Good Friday Agreement in 1998.

'The leadership has formally ordered an end to the armed campaign.'

IRA STATEMENT, JULY 2005

The peace process

The Good Friday Agreement of 1998 paved the way to a devolved assembly where Catholics and Protestants can share power. Northern Ireland is now linked to both the Irish Republic and the UK, but with neither country claiming the province as its own. Instead, Northern Ireland's future is to be decided by a majority of its own people.

Paramilitary prisoners have been released from jail, and there have been reforms to policing and security. But some Protestant politicians have criticised the Agreement, saying they are not satisfied that the IRA has given up armed struggle for ever.

Offshore neighbours

Some parts of the British Isles are neither fully independent, nor fully British. The Channel Islands and the Isle of Man are ancient realms with unusual links to the mainland.

Semi-detached

The Channel Islands, just off the French coast, are leftovers of the period long ago when English kings ruled over the French region of Normandy, and their status reflects this complex history. The islands are crown dependencies, meaning that the British Queen is head of state, although she rules under the title Duke of Normandy, and islanders are entitled to be British citizens. However, the islands themselves are neither part of the United Kingdom, nor members of the European Union. And they are mostly free to form their own treaties with foreign countries, since the UK government only has authority over major issues like defence.

Tax haven

There are five main inhabited Channel islands: Jersey, Guernsey, Alderney, Sark and Herm. Though they share a TV station, almost everything else is done separately, each island having its own legislature, laws and elections. On Sark, decisions are taken by Europe's last remaining feudal overlord, known as the Seigneur. Cars are banned there, while on the even smaller island of Herm, bicycles too are prohibited.

But the islands are perhaps best known for having extremely low rates of income tax, and they have become home to a flourishing banking industry, as well as to those seeking to avoid UK taxes. In order to prevent these people from outnumbering locals, outsiders are only allowed to buy the most expensive properties. Therefore most Britons only see the Channel Islands when taking part in their other big economic activity, which is tourism.

St Peter Port, the capital of Guernsey, is a popular destination for small-boat sailors.

A step back in time

Another tax refuge which has similar relations with the UK is the Isle of Man. Located in the Irish Sea around 96 kilometres from the western coast of Britain, it is an historic treasure. Horse-drawn trams carry people around the capital, Douglas, while elsewhere a steam railway operates, and the parliament, known as the Tynwald, dates back over a thousand years, making it possibly the oldest continuous assembly in the world.

Manx culture is much influenced by the island's Viking and Celtic roots, and the local language, similar to Gaelic, is once again being taught after all but dying out. The Isle of Man also boasts some unique, curious animals including the four-horned 'loaghtan' sheep and the tailless Manx cat.

The TT: festival of speed

Life offshore isn't all about dodging UK tax. The Isle of Man TT is a series of thrilling motorcycle races held every summer (right). Riders compete at up to 200 km/h on a challenging course around the island's winding lanes – which are closed to all other traffic. The event attracts up to 40,000 spectators, and also includes many social activities.

The main inhabited offshore dependencies + area (in sq km) & pop (2003)

Jersey	116	87,186	UK dependency
Guernsey	62	59,807	UK dependency
Herm	2	60	Guernsey dependency
Sark	5	600	Guernsey dependency
Alderney	5	2400	Guernsey dependency
Isle of Man	572	76,315	UK dependency

London: The UK's world city

The English and UK capital is Europe's biggest city and one of the most exciting on Earth. But it is also a city of surprises and challenges.

Centre and suburbs

London is actually two cities in one: the 'Square Mile' of the original City of London, which is now the capital's financial district, and the bigger City of Westminster next door to it – home to the Queen at Buckingham Palace. Around these two centres, another 31 boroughs sprawl. Since 2000 the whole metropolis of more than seven million people has been partly self-governed by an elected mayor and an assembly that sits at a brand new City Hall, near Tower Bridge.

Economic giant

London is the centre of England's legal, media and of course, political establishments. It is also its economic powerhouse. It is so strong economically that some people worry that other parts of the country risk being sidelined. London's historic role as a merchant centre is now reflected in the billions of pounds worth of currency traded daily in the square mile.

London is ideally suited as a hub for trade because, being located at the centre of global time – the Greenwich Meridian – its working day overlaps with both America and the Far East. After hours, the city becomes a major entertainment centre. Its famous theatre district, the West End, also boasts top-class restaurants, nightclubs and bars. Since today's Londoners speak over 300 different languages between them, it is no surprise that many of these have an international flavour.

An evening view of part of the City of London from the south bank of the River Thames with Blackfriars Bridge in the foreground. The dome of St Paul's Cathedral still dominates the City skyline, just as it did when completed by architect Sir Christopher Wren in 1709. Other tall buildings visible are Tower 42 (centre right) and the Swiss-Re building, known popularly as 'The Gherkin' (far right).

'When a man is tired of London, he is tired of life; for there is in London all that life can afford.'
SAMUEL JOHNSON (1709-1784), ENGLISH EIGHTEENTH-CENTURY ESSAYIST

FACTFILE: LONDON

- London is Europe's largest city, with almost 7.2 million people (in 2001) and an area of over 1600 km sq.
- Central London has the highest economic output per head (euro 61,500) of any European Union region
- London provides around 4.5 million jobs
- Over 3 million trips a day are made on the London Underground, and nearly 5.5 million by bus
- There are over 100 theatres in London – more than 50 in the West End alone
- Three-quarters of all foreign visitors to the UK come to London
- London has the UK's tallest building – the 244 m Canary Wharf tower
- London boasts three World Heritage Sites: the Palace and Abbey of Westminster, the Tower of London and Maritime Greenwich
- More than one in three of England's most deprived areas are in London

The hidden side

Despite its size and power though, the capital is in many ways a collection of urban villages. Many small neighbourhoods like Soho and Notting Hill retain an intimate charm, and between them, vast parks offer relief from the noise and traffic. Yet visitors to London might be even more surprised to discover, alongside all the wealth, areas of great poverty too.

Crime, drugs and other social problems blight some districts. And for many people, buying their own home in this expensive city is out of the question. Add to this an ageing transport system, and London's challenges become apparent. One solution might be the Olympic Games, to be held in London in 2012. The authorities hope that this momentous event will spark widespread regeneration, especially in the run-down east of the city.

Ken Livingstone: London's first elected mayor

As brash and outspoken as London itself, Ken Livingstone (below) became the first person to occupy the newly created post of mayor in 2000. Previously known as Red Ken for his left-wing views, he championed minorities and the poor – often at the expense of more wealthy citizens. His many other controversies include attempting to free Trafalgar Square of its famous pigeons and calling US President, George W Bush, the greatest threat to life on earth – just before an official presidential visit. But supporters still felt Mr Livingstone reflected the spirit of London.

Town and country

The UK is densely populated, and changes in the patterns of living are putting a great strain on town and countryside alike – especially in England.

Rush to the countryside

For several decades now, many of England's big towns and cities have been shrinking as hundreds of thousands of people leave for the countryside, hoping for a better quality of life. In particular, almost every one of the past 35 years have seen a drift towards the wealthier southeast of the country, and the effects of such movements have been dramatic. Some older industrial towns are in decline, as their better-off inhabitants move out. While the government is having to plan thousands of new homes elsewhere to accommodate the shifting population – even in areas protected against development, known as green belt. Already, across England, many once-rural areas have become home to new housing estates, roads and giant 'out-of-town' shopping centres.

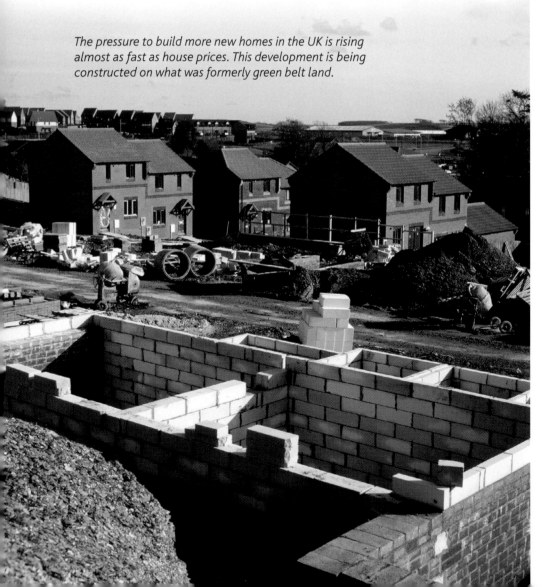

The pressure to build more new homes in the UK is rising almost as fast as house prices. This development is being constructed on what was formerly green belt land.

Rural crisis

These trends have coincided with a decline in agriculture, with the result that the rural way of life is changing fast. Some people fear that traditional villages risk becoming mere 'dormitories', which are empty by day as their new inhabitants commute to work in nearby cities. Many small businesses like farms and village shops have closed. Rural post offices have also been shut down. And when in 2005 the government banned the traditional country sport of hunting foxes with hounds, many critics began to claim that the traditional country way of life was going to disappear forever.

Developing problems

The government wants to meet rising demand for housing in the southeast of England by allowing up to a million new homes to be built there. Many, such as those shown in the picture on the right, will be subsidised so that vital workers like nurses and teachers can afford to live in them. And most will not be built on rural land. But the plans have unleashed a storm of criticism. Campaigners argue that there will not be enough transport, energy or even water for all the new residents. They say the plans will leave a concrete scar across the countryside.

'England could lose most of its real countryside within a single generation.'

CAMPAIGN TO PROTECT RURAL ENGLAND, 2005

Planning for change

Today, the challenge is to accommodate change without altering the face of England – and the rest of the UK – forever. Some people think organic farming could help save cash-strapped farmers. Others claim the countryside must diversify into providing leisure facilities, or growing new crops. Meanwhile, a number of rural authorities have introduced laws to stop outsiders snapping up scarce local property.

There may be some relief in store from the rush to populate the countryside as efforts are being made to improve run-down cities. Converting old, disused industrial buildings into trendy apartments and flats seems to be paying off, and after many years, living in the city might once again be coming back into fashion.

ENGLAND'S HOUSING CRISIS:

Surplus housing supply, 1999 (available dwellings over households needing accommodation)

Northern England: 3.0%	
Midlands: 2.2%	
South: 0.9%	
London: -2.2%	

Expected rise in number of households needing accommodation, 2001-2021:

Northern England: 8.8% (539,000 new households)	
Midlands: 12.1% (478,000 new households)	
South: 18.9% (1,400,000 new households)	
London: 16.5% (517,000 new households)	

Transport: Jam tomorrow

With so many people and so little land, getting about is becoming one of the UK's most difficult problems.

Legacy of neglect

For decades, British governments failed to spend enough money on the nation's transport infrastructure, and today, travellers are paying the price. Unlike most European countries, trains, buses and subways in the UK can be unreliable – despite charging some of the highest fares in the world. The railway network – the world's oldest – is only just recovering from a spate of serious accidents, some caused by rail companies neglecting to maintain the tracks. Even so the government is keen to move even more people and freight off the roads and onto rail. Since 1994, it has had considerable success in doing so.

Clearing the way

Despite this, the roads themselves remain stretched to capacity. Building new ones has become unpopular for environmental reasons. But car ownership has risen steeply across the United Kingdom. In response, the government is planning to lure motorists back onto other forms of transport, using satellite technology to track vehicle movements and charge a fee for each mile driven. In London, drivers already pay a flat fee to enter the city centre at peak times. This has substantially reduced traffic. But politicians elsewhere fear that monitoring drivers' journeys and pricing them out of their cars may be unpopular, so other cities have been slow to adopt their own charging schemes.

Back to the future: trams

One solution to the UK's transport crisis is the reintroduction of trams (above), some 50 years after most cities scrapped them. Less expensive to build than an underground railway and faster than a bus, the tram has the added advantages of being clean, quiet and pleasing to the eye. Manchester, Sheffield and Croydon are among the places that use trams. Dozens of other places are also considering the idea.

The pressure on airports to expand has increased dramatically in the last two decades, mirroring the demand for cheap air travel. Campaigners worry that the enlargement of airports like Stansted in Essex will destroy the countryside forever.

The sky's limits

Surprisingly perhaps, one of the cheapest ways to travel now in the UK can be to fly. Thanks to the emergence of budget carriers, it is possible to fly off for just a few pounds. Some Britons even have second homes overseas, which they commute to at weekends. The growth in air travel though has its own problems. For instance, London is now served by no fewer than five airports, yet even more capacity is needed to meet expected demand. And expanding airports is deeply controversial. Supporters say the UK's economic future depends on it. But critics point out the destruction of countryside and increased pollution it involves. It seems that, for the time being at least, even the skies over the United Kingdom are doomed to suffer traffic jams.

> 'We inherited a creaking transport system: Congested roads and overcrowded trains.'
>
> JOHN PRESCOTT,
> DEPUTY PRIME MINISTER,
> JULY 2000

FACTFILE: TRANSPORT

ROADS (Great Britain)
Motorways: 4353 km
Major roads: 55,918 km
Minor roads: 225,579 km
Number of vehicles registered (2001): 29.7 million
Total road-traffic growth (2004): 1.7%
Estimated road-traffic growth by 2040: 40%

RAILWAYS (Great Britain)
Total rail network: 16,536 km
Amount of network electrified: 4928 km (29.8%)
Passenger km travelled (2004): 41.6 billion
Journeys made per day (2004): 2,820,000

AIR
Number of passengers (2002): 189 million
Number of passengers predicted (2030): 476 million
Average growth per year: 4.25%
Number of foreign holidays taken by UK residents per year: 41 million

OTHER
Average number of bicycle trips per person per year (2004): 15
Average bicycle kilometres travelled per person per year (2004): 58 km
Average distance walked per person per year (2001): 304 km

Health: The costs of living

The UK was at the forefront of twentieth-century health and welfare provision, but today, it is having to change the way it looks after itself.

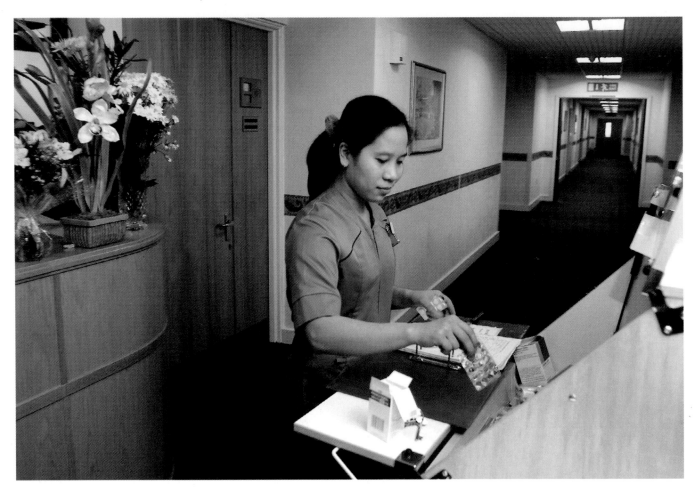

Inside a privately run hospital. More and more people with health problems choose to 'go private', instead of waiting for treatment on the National Health Service.

The state steps in

After World War II, the British government introduced an extensive welfare system which provided free care for everyone, regardless of income, from the cradle to the grave. The crowning glory of this so-called welfare state was the National Health Service (NHS), where even the poorest citizens could see a doctor and get treatment. The NHS has since become one of the nation's best-loved institutions – and one of the most expensive. In the year 2005, for example, it cost £76 billion to run.

Plugging the gap

One problem is that the UK's people are now living longer than ever before. This means that the cost of medicines and operations is rising, as more patients grow old and frail. Today, with a huge investment programme underway, more taxpayers' money than ever is being spent on the NHS. But even this is not enough. So the Service is trying to find the extra funds needed by teaming up with private companies to build new hospitals and even to provide some treatments. Not everyone approves of the idea, because they are so attached to the NHS and fear that introducing profit-making companies into the system may weaken its basic principle of being free to use.

Putting on weight: the UK's fat problem

The UK is better than ever at treating the unwell, but in some respects it is still becoming more unhealthy. Obesity (as in picture, right) has trebled in the last 20 years, thanks to more car use, richer food, and fewer people doing heavy manual work. By 2010, one-quarter of all adults could be dangerously overweight, spelling up to £4 billion in additional health costs. Obese people are more likely to develop heart disease, diabetes and high blood pressure.

'We expect more from our health care system than ever.'
HEALTH THINK-TANK, THE KING'S FUND, 2004

Prevention not cure

At the same time, the health authorities are trying to encourage people to look after themselves better and not to get ill in the first place. In particular, they have introduced measures to encourage more healthy eating habits, and – since only a minority of Britons now smoke – to ban smoking in public places.

Alcohol abuse, too, has become a big issue. One-third of British men and one-fifth of women drink more than they should, and 22,000 people a year die because of alcohol-related illnesses.

Alcohol abuse causes other problems, too. For example, many people get involved in crimes and violence through being drunk. The government is especially worried about alcohol abuse among young people. But one of its solutions – to extend the hours in which alcohol can be consumed in pubs, bars and clubs – is proving controversial. Ministers believe it encourages people to drink more slowly and responsibly. But opponents worry that it will lead to a massive increase in consumption, and even more illness.

FACTFILE : HEALTH COSTS AND BENEFITS

NHS spending (1997-8):	£40 billion
NHS spending (2005-6):	£76 billion
Projected NHS spending (2007-8):	£93 billion

Number of NHS employees	1,300,000
Average cost of a doctor (2004-5)	£83,000pa
Average cost of a nurse (2004-5)	£24,534pa
NHS funding deficit (2005-6):	£620 million

Waiting list for hospital treatment (1997):	1,158,000
Waiting list for hospital treatment (2004):	857,000

In 2003-04 the NHS provided:-
- 325 million consultations with doctors or nurses
- 13.3 million outpatient consultations
- 5.4 million planned hospital admissions
- 4.2 million emergency hospital admissions

Leisure: Tradition and adventure

The UK's favourite pastime is, unsurprisingly, watching television. But beyond that, the nation enjoys a wealth of recreation.

Staying in

Most people in the UK work a five-day week, Monday to Friday, so weekends are the main time for entertainment. This trend may even have increased in recent years, as the laws restricting trading on Sundays have been relaxed, due to a fall in churchgoing. Yet, in this house-proud land, the home, as well as the public sphere, is a major leisure arena. A recent EU survey found that the most popular pursuit after watching TV is visiting friends to eat and drink. Other domestic activities include gardening and carrying out home improvements.

> 'All work and no play makes Jack a dull boy.'
> ENGLISH PROVERB

The British public house has traditionally been at the heart of a neighbourhood; a place for socialising as well as drinking.

New tastes

When people do go out, many still visit that unique British institution, the public house, or pub. The pub is a place for talking to strangers, getting to know the owner, and playing games or even sports. Pub-going though is facing competition. For one thing, the UK has discovered food. Scores of different cuisines are now available in almost any big town or city. Such is the fondness for Indian food, for example, that a popular variety of curry was recently voted as the UK's true national dish.

In the field of culture, cinema is the biggest attraction, but theatre, dance and live music also draw in the crowds. And visits to public art galleries and museums have almost doubled since the government abolished entrance fees, several years ago. The arts benefit from grants provided by the UK National Lottery.

Rugby is one of UK's most popular sports for TV viewing. For participating though, walking comes out on top.

On the field

The pastime about which the UK is perhaps the most passionate of all, however, is sport. Football and rugby are played in all four countries, while in England and some parts of Wales, cricket also predominates in summer. England's 2003 rugby world cup triumph, and its victory over the Australians in the 2005 Ashes series, have boosted interest in both. And it is hoped that the Olympic Games, to be held in London in 2012, will boost participation in sport more generally.

The BBC: broadcasting legend

The British Broadcasting Corporation, or BBC, is one of the world's largest providers of radio, television and internet content. Dating back to 1922, it began the first-ever regular TV service in 1936, and its programmes are still seen as among the best. They are also free of advertisements – free because the BBC is funded by a yearly licence that, by law, all television owners must buy. A staunchly independent news-provider, BBC journalists have attracted the displeasure of British and foreign governments alike.

FACTFILE: LEISURE

Average time spent watching television each day:
Males: 2 hours 45 minutes
Females: 2 hours 25 minutes

Average time spent doing housework each day:
Males: 1 hour 40 minutes
Females: 3 hours

Visits to the cinema (2004): 171 million
Number of households with internet access (2005): 12.9 million

Top tourist attractions, 2001 (with visitor numbers in millions)
Blackpool pleasure beach (6.5); National Gallery, London (4.9); British Museum, London (4.8); Tate Modern art gallery, London (3.6); Tower of London (2.0); York Minster, York, and Legoland, Windsor (1.6 each)

Most popular sports (with percentage of adults taking part)
Walking/rambling (70); Swimming (27); Keep fit (23); Snooker/pool (19); Cycling (18); Weight training (12); Fishing (11); Football (10)

Education: Put to the test

Education is changing rapidly in the UK today, as the government aims to provide a better education for more youngsters. But not everyone agrees on the best way to do this.

Top class

Not all UK schools are the same. Some, known as public schools, are in fact privately run; they receive little or no government money, and parents pay fees instead. However, most children attend a state-funded school.

Today, these are changing, because the government wants them to have more control over their own affairs. Failing schools, for example, can be closed and replaced by schools with the support of local businesses, or religious and community groups. Critics say the sponsors get too much influence over what children are taught. But ministers say they bring specialist knowledge and help provide brand new facilities at a lower cost to taxpayers.

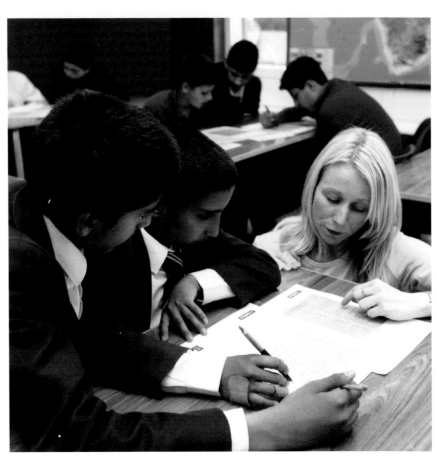

The schools system has been a top priority of recent UK governments.

Paying to learn

The schooling and exam system differs in England and Wales, Scotland and Northern Ireland. At age 18 though, a growing number of children throughout the UK now go to college or university. This normally involves moving away from home for the first time. In recent years, studying at university has become much more expensive. Many students do not receive a grant to cover living expenses, and also have to pay some of their tuition fees. Special government loans are available to cover these costs. The loans do not have to be repaid until the student has graduated and begun work.

'Ask me my three main priorities for government, and I tell you: education, education, education.'

TONY BLAIR,
BRITISH PRIME MINISTER-TO-BE,
OCTOBER, 1996

EDUCATION FACT FILE:

Enrolments to higher education courses (2002-3): 2,175,115 (up 4.3%)

MIXED ACHIEVEMENTS:

Percentage of qualified workforce by region (2003)
Which regions of the UK perform best?

	Degree or equiv.	GCSE A-C or equiv.	None
UK as a whole	**16.3**	**21.7**	**15.0**
England / northeast	11.3	22.7	18.8
England / West Midlands	12.7	22.7	17.6
London	24.7	16.7	13.4
England / southeast	19.9	22.4	10.6
Wales	14.6	23.4	17.1
Scotland	15.4	16.4	14.7
Northern Ireland	13.1	21.0	23.7

THE BENEFITS OF LEARNING (2003 figures)

Average income for employees qualified to degree level: £632pw
Average income for employees with no qualifications: £298pw
Number of adults qualified to degree level in full-time employment: 88%
Number of adults with no qualifications in full-time employment: 50%

The Open University

The UK's biggest university has no traditional campus and you don't need to pass any exams to get in. The Open University, established in the 1960s, aims to provide degree and post-graduate courses to anyone, regardless of their academic background. Students learn by attending seminars near to where they live or work, and through specially made radio and TV programmes. Many of them are older people who missed out on university when they left school. The university currently has around 150,000 undergraduates and 30,000 post-graduate students.

Could do better

By 2010, the government wants half of all school-leavers to continue studying at college or university. But media studies, psychology and sociology are increasingly popular, while sciences and languages are often overlooked. Some business leaders believe that today's graduates lack the skills that the UK needs, especially in areas like engineering and high technology. They argue that many young people would be better off taking vocational courses, apprenticeships or simply starting work instead.

A pupil performs an experiment in a secondary-school laboratory. There is concern that not enough UK students choose science-based university courses.

Resources: Running on empty

For centuries, the UK has enjoyed food and energy to spare. But many of its natural resources are now growing more scarce.

Black gold

Compared to the rest of Europe, the UK has relatively little woodland and few mineral resources. However, few other countries on the continent have as much oil or gas to exploit. Huge lakes of oil beneath the North Sea were first tapped in 1975, and by the 1990s, the UK had become one of the world's top ten producers, producing up to one-fifth of its own needs and generating impressive export revenues. Today, powerful rigs continue to drill the seabed off the shores of eastern Scotland, piping oil and natural gas back to the mainland. But this output has now reached its peak, and is expected to decline in years to come.

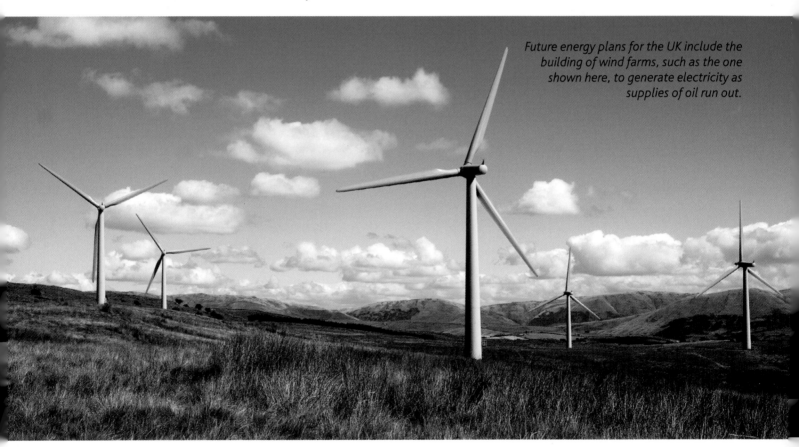

Future energy plans for the UK include the building of wind farms, such as the one shown here, to generate electricity as supplies of oil run out.

Renewable riches

The coal industry is already in decline, despite enormous reserves still lying beneath the British countryside. Cheap imports are mainly to blame, although demand is also falling because the government wants to encourage the use of cleaner forms of energy that do not contribute to global warming. Here, the UK's notoriously poor weather may come into its own, because there are plans to build huge wind farms. These will harness the power of nature to generate electricity. The waves lapping UK coastlines, too, may one day be used for this purpose. In the meantime, the government is considering a new generation of nuclear power stations to help fill the gap left by coal, oil and gas.

The foot-and-mouth disease outbreak in 2001-2 resulted in thousands of animals having to be killed and burned.

Land of plenty?

The UK's edible resources, too, are facing problems. Around three-quarters of the land is suitable for agriculture, and almost half of that can be used to grow crops. The best arable land is in southern and eastern England and eastern Scotland, while most of the rest can be used to keep livestock. Despite this, the UK imports almost half its food from abroad. And recent health scares like foot-and-mouth disease and BSE (mad cow disease) have not helped its farmers.

Meanwhile the fishing industry, once stronger than most, is now facing ruin thanks to depleted fish stocks and stiff competition from European neighbours. It seems that, while the UK could once rely on natural resources for its wealth, in a less plentiful future it will instead have to look to its most promising asset of all for survival : the ideas and ingenuity of its people.

'An island of coal surrounded by a sea of fish.'
ANEURIN BEVAN (1897-1960), GOVERNMENT MINISTER, 1945

'An island of creativity surrounded by a sea of understanding.'
SIR DAVID PUTTNAM, GOVERNMENT ADVISER, 1996

FACTFILE: RESOURCES

Electricity production (2003):
From gas: 38%
From coal: 35%
From nuclear power: 22%
From oil: 1%
Others: 4%

Oil: Dwindling reserves, rising prices
Total estimated reserves (and estimated value)
2004: 3.0 bn tonnes (£63.4bn)
2000: 3.8 bn tonnes (£51.7 bn)
1995: 4.8 bn tonnes (£38.7bn)

UK oil consumption: 1.76 million barrels per day (approx 282 million litres)

Land use, millions of hectares (1998):		
Developed land:	1.8	(7.7%)
Semi-natural land:	7.0	(29.8%)
Intensive agriculture:	10.8	(46%)
Woodland:	2.8	(11.9%)
Other:	1.1	(4.6%)

The UK tomorrow

The old certainties of empire, industry and British national identity no longer hold true for the United Kingdom, and with their passing, the nation faces some daunting challenges.

Together or alone?

The UK faces many difficulties. Housing shortages, an outdated transport system and environmental problems to name but a few. The biggest consideration though, may well be the political question of whether the United Kingdom continues to exist at all, or whether England, Scotland, Wales and Northern Ireland decide at some future point to go their own separate ways. Some people believe that devolution has already started this process.

The other big political issue is the UK's place within the European Union. There is growing demand for the government to reject closer relations with other EU countries. But many businesses and pro-Europeans say the UK will find it difficult to survive unless it makes the most of these links.

Young and old

At home, the size and nature of the population is likely to pose some challenges too. With so many people living longer than ever before, healthcare and pensions will become a greater burden on the state. There is serious concern that younger people are not saving enough money now to pay for their own retirement. Meanwhile, the extent of immigration to the UK worries some people, while others say that it is the only way to get the skilled and unskilled workers that the economy needs. Without it, they add, there may not be enough taxpayers to meet the costs of the growing retired population.

One of the most hotly debated political issues in the UK today is greater integration within the EU, including the adoption of the Euro currency.

Working smarter

The kind of work that people do is also likely to change. The UK will probably make fewer manufactured goods, and will concentrate on providing services instead, so people will work with their brains rather than their hands.

Perhaps it is in this sphere that the best hopes lie, since the British are an original, inventive and resourceful nation. In recent years they have proved that they can turn away from dwelling on a glorious past and look to the future with confidence. In the United Kingdom today, the future may look tough. But the nation's record of energy, creativity and open-mindedness suggests that, one way or another, it will continue to prosper.

The cost of healthcare to look after a population that is living longer will be a major social consideration in the United Kingdom's future.

FUTURE TRENDS: A CHANGING SOCIETY

Take a look at the following changes which took place over the 35 years between 1971 and 2003. What do they tell us about what kind of country the UK is likely to become in the future?

- The UK's population increased by 6% (3.6 million), but the number of separate households increased by 32%
- The number of people buying their own houses increased from 9.6 million to 18.1 million
- The average age of a UK citizen increased from 34.1 to 38.4
- Children living in lone-parent families tripled to 24%
- Male employment decreased from 92% to 79%, but female employment increased from 56% to 70%
- Spending on recreation and culture increased sixfold to £84 billion
- The proportion of obese adults increased from 14.5% (in 1993) to 23% in 2003

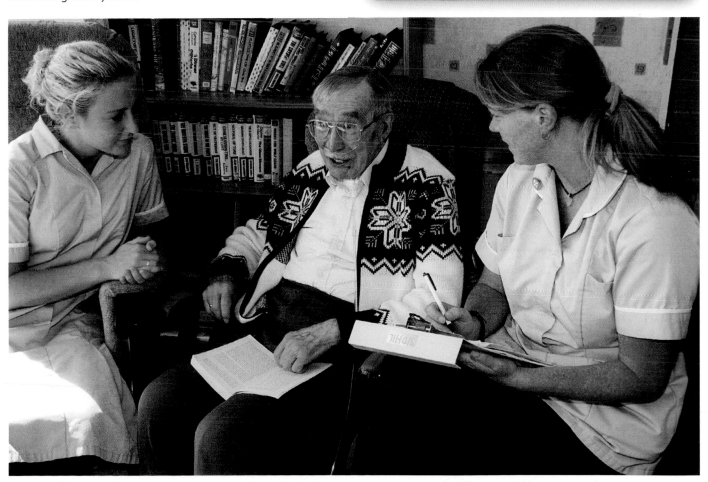

Timeline of UK events

1066: William, Duke of Normandy, invades England and becomes king.

1170-5: English king, Henry II, conquers Ireland.

1282: Welsh prince Llywelyn defeated by English king, Edward I. Wales under English control.

1536: King Henry VIII passes Act of Union that makes Wales part of England.

1603: Queen Elizabeth I of England dies. James Stuart (King James VI of Scotland) becomes King James I of England and Scotland.

1642-59: Civil wars wreak havoc in England and Wales, Scotland and Ireland. James's son, Charles I executed in 1649. England becomes a republic.

1660: Restoration of the monarchy. Charles II becomes king.

1688: Charles's Catholic brother James II gives up the throne. His Protestant daughter Mary and her husband William of Orange rule jointly.

1707: Act of Union under Mary's sister Queen Anne unites Scottish and English parliaments. The United Kingdom created.

1714: Queen Anne dies leaving no heirs; she is succeeded by her cousin George, Elector of Hanover, who becomes George I.

1715: Rebellion in Scotland attempts to restore the Catholic Stuart family to the throne.

1745: Second rebellion ('the 45') in Scotland led by 'Bonnie Prince Charlie' again tries to restore the Stuart monarchy. It is crushed at the Battle of Culloden, 1746.

1793: Wars with France begin; UK threatened with invasion by French forces. France eventually defeated in 1815 at the Battle of Waterloo.

1802: Act of Union brings Ireland into the United Kingdom.

1832: Reform Bills reorganise the way the UK is governed. Further bills follow in 1867, 1884 and 1885.

1870: Education Act makes children's education compulsory and sets up state schools.

1900: British Empire at its most powerful.

1914-18: World War I; Britain fights on the side of the Allies; nearly 660,000 men killed.

1916: Easter Rising in Ireland. Irish Free State set up in 1922; Northern Ireland's six counties remain part of the UK.

1918: Women granted the vote in the UK for the first time.

1939-45: World War II. Britain again fights on the Allied side. UK cities and towns bombed.

1946-51: Many UK industries – such as coal and transport – nationalised by Labour government.

1947 onwards: British colonies and territories granted independence.

1948: National Health Service set up.

1950s onwards: Waves of immigration dramatically change make-up of UK society.

1969 onwards: Troubles in Northern Ireland.

1979-97: Conservative government privatises former nationalised industries; extends home and share ownership.

1997: Reforming Labour government elected. Re-elected in 2001 and 2005.

1998: Scottish parliament and Welsh assembly set up.

1998: Good Friday Agreement in Northern Ireland.

2005: IRA renounces violence in Northern Ireland.

Glossary and websites

Angles   Germanic tribesmen who settled in Britain in the 5th century

Catholic/Roman Catholic   Member of the Christian church that recognises the Pope as its spiritual leader

Celts   A prehistoric European people, with shared language and culture

Commonwealth   The community of states and dependencies once part of the British Empire

Cymru   The Welsh word for Wales (pronounced 'Kumry')

Devolution   The process by which the government in London passes on some of its powers to smaller regional bodies, such as the Scottish parliament

European Union   A grouping of European states which provides economic, commercial and cultural links, and aims to bring all its members ever closer together

Great Britain   The eighth largest island in the world. It is home to the three separate countries of England, Scotland and Wales

Greenwich Meridian   Zero degrees longitude – the point from which the world's time zones are calculated

Head of State   A country's main public representative, such as its king, queen, or president

Hereditary monarch   A king or queen who inherits the throne from another member of their family

Hunter-gatherers   People who live entirely by hunting and foraging for food, without any settled agriculture

Highlands   Mountainous region of northern Scotland, known for its great scenic beauty

Loch   A lake or inlet of the sea in Scotland

Luddite   One of a group of early nineteenth-century English workmen who destroyed labour-saving machinery, which had caused them to lose their means of making a living

National Health Service (NHS)   The UK's public health system, paid for by taxes rather than doctors' fees

Nonconformist   Protestant religion or worshipper that does not accept the authority of the Church of England

Normans   People from Normandy in northern France, who conquered England in 1066, replacing the Angles and Saxons as rulers

Organic farming   Producing crops and livestock without the use of chemicals and drugs

Papacy   The office of the Pope, leader of the Roman Catholic Church

Paramilitary   A member of one of the armed groups which adopted military-style tactics to wage campaigns of violence in Northern Ireland

Protestant   A follower of one of the Christian groups which split from the Roman Catholic Church in the sixteenth century

Romans   The people of ancient Rome, who built a mighty empire in Europe, and conquered most of Britain in 43 CE

Saxons   A war-like people from what is now northwestern Germany, who settled in Britain after the collapse of the Roman Empire

United Kingdom   The state formed by the union of England, Scotland, Wales and Northern Ireland

www.direct.gov.uk Website of the UK government

www.parliament.uk Official website of the Houses of Parliament

www.scottish.parliament.uk Official website of the Scottish parliament

www.wales.gov.uk Welsh assembly website

www.niassembly.gov.uk Website of the Northern Ireland assembly

www.london.gov.uk Website for the Mayor of London & London Assembly

www.statistics.gov.uk Facts and figures from UK census and other official sources

www.bbc.co.uk British Broadcasting Corporation homepage: links to historical and factual information about the UK, news and radio and television programmes

www.visitbritain.com Tourist information and features (multilingual)

Map

COUNTIES OF ENGLAND
(and main administrative centres)

Bedfordshire (Bedford),
Berkshire (Reading),
Buckinghamshire (Aylesbury),
Cambridgeshire (Cambridge),
Cheshire (Chester), Cornwall (Truro),
Cumbria (Carlisle),
Derbyshire (Matlock), Devon (Exeter),
Dorset (Dorchester), Durham (Durham),
East Riding of Yorkshire (Beverley),
East Sussex (Lewes), Essex (Chelmsford),
Gloucestershire (Gloucester),
Greater London, Greater Manchester,
Hampshire (Winchester),
Herefordshire (Hereford),
Hertfordshire (Hertford),
Isle of Wight (Newport),
Kent (Maidstone), Lancashire (Preston),
Leicestershire (Leicester),
Lincolnshire (Lincoln),
Merseyside (Liverpool),
Norfolk (Norwich),
Northamptonshire (Northampton),
Northumberland (Newcastle upon Tyne),
North Yorkshire (Northallerton),
Nottinghamshire (Nottingham),
Oxfordshire (Oxford),
Rutland (Oakham),
Shropshire (Shrewsbury),
Somerset (Taunton),
South Yorkshire (Barnsley),
Staffordshire (Stafford),
Suffolk (Ipswich),
Surrey (Kingston upon Thames),
Tyne and Wear (Newcastle),
Warwickshire (Warwick),
West Midlands (Birmingham),
West Sussex (Chichester),
West Yorkshire (Wakefield),
Wiltshire (Trowbridge),
Worcestershire (Worcester)

SCOTTISH COUNCILS

Aberdeen City, Aberdeenshire, Angus,
Argyll and Bute, Clackmannanshire,
Dumfries and Galloway, Dundee City,
East Ayrshire, East Dunbartonshire,
East Lothian, East Renfrewshire,
Edinburgh City, Eilean Siar, Falkirk, Fife,
Glasgow City, Highland, Inverclyde,
Midlothian, Moray, North Ayrshire,
North Lanarkshire, Orkney Islands,
Perth and Kinross, Renfrewshire,
Scottish Borders, Shetland Islands,
South Ayrshire, South Lanarkshire,
Stirling, West Dunbartonshire,
West Lothian

WELSH COUNCILS

Blaenau Gwent, Bridgend, Caerphilly,
Cardiff, Carmarthenshire, Ceredigion,
Conwy, Denbighshire, Flintshire, Gwynedd,
Isle of Anglesey, Merthyr Tydfil,
Monmouthshire, Neath Port Talbot,
Newport, Pembrokeshire, Powys,
Rhondda Cynon Taff, Swansea, Torfaen,
Vale of Glamorgan, Wrexham

COUNTIES OF NORTHERN IRELAND

Antrim, Armagh, Down, Fermanagh,
Londonderry/Derry, Tyrone

Index